INTRODUCTION

The object of this little book is to produce a short but interesting record of places, people and events in and around Freshwater during the period from 1880-1930.

Many treatises have been written about the Island and its past, which are readily available from local libraries. To write specifically about a village and its neighbours could best be achieved by a local person, not too old to forget and not too young to remember.

I hope that the presentation of these few pictures may recall some of the stories passed on by parents and grandparents. I would like to convey grateful thanks to my many friends for the generosity in allowing me the use of their cherished possessions.

Joy Lester, Freshwater Bay, I.W. 1983

Freshwater

in old picture postcards

by
Joyce E. Lester

European Library - Zaltbommel/Netherlands MCMLXXXIII

GB   ISBN 90 288 2318 2

European Library in Zaltbommel/Netherlands publishes among other things the following series:

IN OLD PICTURE POSTCARDS *is a series of books which sets out to show what a particular place looked like and what life was like in Victorian and Edwardian times. A book about virtually every town in the United Kingdom is to be published in this series. By the end of this year about 75 different volumes will have appeared. 1,250 books have already been published devoted to the Netherlands with the title* **In oude ansichten.** *In Germany, Austria and Switzerland 500, 60 and 15 books have been published as* **In alten Ansichten;** *in France by the name* **En cartes postales anciennes** *and in Belgium as* **En cartes postales anciennes** *and/or* **In oude prentkaarten** *150 respectively 400 volumes have been published.*

For further particulars about published or forthcoming books, apply to your bookseller or direct to the publisher.

This edition has been printed and bound by Grafisch Bedrijf De Steigerpoort in Zaltbommel/Netherlands.

1. Freshwater Bay circa 1897. This picture of the Bay shows the old promenade, but in 1899 there occurred wholesale wreckage of the sea wall and esplanade during the recent storms. This led to much discussion as to remedial measures to prevent the continued encroachment of the sea and danger of the isolation of the Western Wight. However, when the Poet Tennyson first came to Freshwater Bay, meadow and down stretched unbroken to the edge of the beach. The Albion Hotel, standing in its unrivalled position, attracts many visitors, some of whom return year after year to enjoy the ever changing moods of the Bay and to witness the beautiful colours created by the sun when it rises above the Arch and Stag rocks in the early morning. (Photo A.H. Kirk.)

2. Freshwater Bay circa 1896. Looking across the Bay to Tennyson Down one can just make out the old Beacon and below, on the cliff, the old Fort Redoubt, which was built about 1856. To the right of the fort stands the old Freshwater Bay Hotel showing the new third storey extension and below the hotel, situated on the sea wall, was an interesting Marine Bathing House, where the less hardy and more modest could bathe. In more recent years it was referred to as 'The Bath House' and was used as changing rooms – 6d. upstairs and 3d. downstairs – until it was finally demolished about 1950. (Photo A.H. Kirk.)

3. View from Government Road, Freshwater Bay, circa 1908. This road, having been known as Military Road for many years, was built during the Crimean War. When fears of an invasion became remote, the road was allowed to become a series of farm tracks ten miles long. It was not long before a disagreement with France created fresh fears and once again the road was rendered fit for the transport of troops and guns; these fears also coming to an abrupt end and by degrees the road relapsed again into becoming farm tracks. This procedure was repeated several times, the last taking place early in 1915 when enemy reports claimed that 'the Isle-of-Wight has been captured' thus giving rise to further fears of an invasion. Eventually the Council took control of the stretch of road, but problems are now arising with the erosion of the cliffs, bringing a section of the road perilously near the edge which could, in the future, cause possible closure. The house 'Sea View' in the foreground of the picture with the marquee in the garden is no longer with us, having been buried under the car park about ten years ago.

4. St. Agnes Church, Freshwater Bay circa 1909. This pretty little church is of no great age, for it was built seventy-five years ago, to replace a building known as the 'Iron Room', which stood in the Square and had become unsuitable for worship owing to the increased population and the number of visitors. The Reverend A.J. Robertson was rector at the time and immediate action followed the presentation of the site by Hallam Lord Tennyson, son of the late Poet Laureate. The stones and tiles are genuinely old, having been taken from an ancient farmhouse, which stood on Hook Hill – the hill leading to the Parish Church. The porch was the gift of Lady Tennyson, as a memorial to her mother, who also suggested the new church should be dedicated to St. Agnes as she had always admired the young and beautiful Saint. The foundation stone was laid by Harold Tennyson in April 1908 and the work completed, apart from the thatched roof for which Norfolk reeds were used, in the following August and on the twelfth day of the same month the church was dedicated by Dr. Ryle, the then Bishop of Winchester.

5. Freshwater Bay — Bathing Tents and Parade circa 1906. By this time the promenade has been restored after the ravages of the 1899 storms, the Bay now becoming quite a popular resort. A new slipway had been incorporated with the rebuilding, where railings had been erected nearby the Albion Hotel. This slipway provided better facilities for the boatmen and for the manoeuvring of bathing machines. In 1890 the Prince and Princess of Battenberg visited the Bay and received an address at the Regatta, which was inaugurated on their Royal Highnesses' marriage.

6. Freshwater Bay — Bathing Beach circa 1906. Showing the eastern end of the promenade towards the Arch and Stag rocks. The house 'Glenbrook', later known as 'Glenbrook St. Francis', was once the home of Lady Tennyson, the wife of the second Lord Tennyson, who as May Princep featured in many of Mrs. Julia Margaret Cameron's photographs. During the early part of the 1914-1918 War, Lady Tennyson started and supervised the Afton Red Cross Hospital, where some fifteen hundred patients had been admitted. It is interesting to note in the picture the amount of sand in the Bay compared with the beach today.

7. Early on September 29th, 1905 a serious fire destroyed the old Standard Inn, School Green, Freshwater. Mr. Walter Scorey was occupier at the time and he and other occupants managed to escape safely. To the left of the stricken premises there was a Blacksmith's Shop where later the Gaiety Theatre was built. The newer looking building operated as 'Warehams Art Potteries'. Strange that it should be so close to the existing Pottery Studio, which was established approximately two hundred yards to the east in 1953 after nearly fifty years.

8. London House, Freshwater circa 1920. This old established business was situated in Queen's Road, opposite the site of the old fire station and the footpath leading through Spinfish to Sheepwash and Middleton. The shop had many departments and in addition to those displayed on the building, stocked according to an 1883 advertisement, Brussels, Tapestry, Kidderminster and Hemp Carpets, together with sewing machines and paper hangings 'at wholesale prices'. Inside a 'modern' payment system had been installed, whereby overhead wires ran to a central cash desk from all departments. The assistant would place the customers money and bill in a container, attach it to the runner, pull the lever and away it would go, returning after a few minutes with the change. The business, known to later generations as 'Shannons', closed down about the 1940's. However the building has since been restored and is currently occupied by 'Isle-of-Wight Glass'.

9. Farringford circa 1898. This lovely picture of Farringford is as it looked when the Poet Alfred Lord Tennyson lived there — surrounded by many different varieties of trees and shrubs. The face of the house, with the great magnolia and roses twining round the windows of Tennyson's own special rooms, remained almost the same for many years after the poet's death in 1892. The house remained in the Tennyson family until after the Second World War, when it was finally sold and became known as the Farringford Hotel. However, one may still visit the poet's study and trace his footsteps along the lanes around, following the path to the downs he loved so much; where on a dull and misty day and with a vivid imagination one may even see a tall figure wearing a black cloak and a large black hat emerge from the mist only to disappear again! (Photo A.H. Kirk.)

10. Tennyson's Bridge circa 1897. This attractive little rustic bridge was a most ingenious device of the poet to secure the privacy for which he craved, without contravening the law of the land. There was a short right of way running through the Farringford Estate where strangers used to prowl, approaching him with their greetings and questions. Tennyson set to work and lowered the level of the lane, where it crossed the path he used for his daily walks and then bridged the gap above. Thereafter, a glimpse of a tall figure striding rapidly overhead was all the visitor could hope for and these glimpses are, supposedly, still seen today! (Photo A.J. Kirk.)

11. Freshwater Railway Station circa 1910. This was the last line of the network of the Island Railways to be opened for passengers on 20th July 1889 'for the convenience of the people living in the West Wight'. The carriages outside the station carried visitors to the local hotels in which they had chosen to stay; as one can observe it was quite a busy terminus and a great asset to Freshwater. It was a single line track and sometimes on the way to Newport the driver would stop his train and pop over the nearby farm to collect his eggs — all heads leaning out of the windows of the train, wondering what was going on. When the railway closed down in 1955, it was a sad blow for Freshwater and district and many businesses suffered. On the arrival of the midday train during the season, dozens of visitors walked from the station and through the village on their way to Colwell Bay — thus patronising the local shops. There is a little booklet entitled 'The Great Isle-of-Wight Train Robbery', which is most interesting.

12. The War Knight came to rest off Watcombe Bay, Freshwater on the 5th April 1918 after having struck a mine. She had previously been in collision with another vessel whilst in convoy out in the Channel. War Knight, a 'Merchantman', carried a mixed cargo which included rubber, barrels of oil, pork and boxes of lard. Much of this was washed ashore at Freshwater Bay. Needless to say the Bay was alive with activity and it was a free for all before the goods were salvaged by the Authorities and sold locally. Unfortunately, there were a number of court cases for not having declared the wreck and one woman, when questioned, was found to have three legs of pork concealed in her chimney; she also had some boxes of lard, but was dealt with leniently after pleading she had six children to feed — her fine was 15/-. Strangely enough, after sixty-five years the stricken vessel has just given up another bale of rubber which came ashore at Freshwater Bay — a reminder of the First World War.

13. Freshwater National School, Group IV circa 1915. The children do not look very happy, do they? This school, built of natural stone, dates from 1850, the pupils having been transferred from their humble beginnings at Moa Place School Green, which consisted of two thatched cottages in a poor state of repair. The new school had a master's house attached, where one can see the tin bath hanging on the wall. This was brought into the house on Saturday night for the usual weekly bath, taking place in front of the kitchen fire! In more recent times the school has always been referred to as 'All Saint's'.

14. The Drill Hall circa 1915. The new Drill Hall in Freshwater was erected in 1899 for the Artillery Volunteers as a memorial to Mrs. Cameron, the well known lady photographer, who subscribed £100. The building cost about £900 and was opened by Col. Sir Charles Seely, another generous supporter of the building fund; Lord Tennyson having laid the foundation stone. After the Second World War the Drill Hall was made redundant and in about 1961 the Freshwater and Totland Parish Councils purchased the property. It was finally converted into the Memorial Hall, as it stands today, for the benefit of the local community.

15. Old Mill Freshwater circa 1880. This mill stood in the field off Windmill Lane, which leads off from Summers Lane. Following the grassy path around the windmill brought one to a house called The Hawkridge, where at that time lived a niece of Lord Tennyson, named Mrs. Agnes Grace Weld. When the mill was demolished the stone was used in the building of 'Stonewind Farmhouse' nearby. The existence of this windmill is marked on the early Island maps.

Orchard's Stores, Freshwater Bay, I.W.

16. Orchard Bros., circa 1930, proudly presenting their new vans, which had replaced the horse drawn vehicles used for deliveries. This building was erected circa 1845 and prior to Mr. Orchard opening his business in 1865 the house had been a private dwelling. To the left was the bakehouse and to the right the Post Office, of which Mr. Orchard was Post Master. Later the office included a branch agency for Waterhouse & Co., of Totland and a branch of Lloyd's Bank. Apart from grocery and provisions, other commodities were stocked, such as oil, coal, wines and spirits. Many well known people were customers and at one time Poets Tennyson and Longfellow were in the shop together. Inside the shop, which is still in the hands of the Orchard family, there hangs an interesting clock, which in 1900 was presented to Orchard Bros., for winning the 'best baked Hovis' competition in the South. The baker at the time was a Mr. Harding, who received a gold medallion. Instead of numerals the five minute sections spell the words 'Hovis Bread' and after eighty-three years the clock is 'still going strong' and keeping good time.

17. Pound Green Freshwater circa 1906. Alongside Farringford Lodge runs a footpath known as 'Granny's mead', leading to Pound Green. Granny Groves who was ninety-four in 1864, lived on the Farringford Estate – from whom, maybe, the footpath acquired its name. In the picture one can see the white wall of the pound into which straying cattle were driven. The ivy clad pound still stands on the green having been well maintained. Some of the cottages around the green still remain. One of particular interest is the charming little seventeenth century Lea Cottage. It was here that Mary Hillier was born in 1847 and became a personal maid to Julia Margaret Cameron of Dimbola Lodge, Freshwater Bay, featuring in many of her photographs. Mrs. Cameron was always careful in choosing her maids for their looks.

18. School Green circa 1906. Children on their way to the National School, which was situated about a hundred yards along the road ahead. The little thatched cottage called 'Oak Cottage' was built in 1794, but was unfortunately destroyed by fire around 1909. The three houses shown had already been turned into shops and later further shops were built alongside taking in the site of the burnt out cottage. These new buildings were similar in design. One opened as Miss Newbold's Millinery Shop, the middle one as Lithgow's Bakery and the third was McClellons photographic studio. During the early part of the 1914-1918 War this studio was completely wrecked having been struck by a shell, which ricocheted after being fired from one of the western forts. Happily there were no casualties.

19. Colwell Common from Gorse Hill circa 1912. The gentleman with his bicycle is Mr. Schwind, a well known resident and owner of the London House Drapery store and outfitters. In the distance is Colwell Bay Inn and a little way beyond is the Baptist Chapel, which was rebuilt and enlarged about 1914. Alongside one of the outer walls there is a headstone in memory of 'Sheppie Paul' as he was known, who for many years tended the sheep on the lush Tennyson Downs. 'Sheppie Paul' lived in a little cottage at the foot of the downs and although only receiving half-a-crown a week managed to save and was able to leave an endowment for the poor children of Freshwater to help with their Apprenticeships. The white cottage to the left is Rockstone Cottage, built in 1790 and now a Private Hotel. The left hand finger of the signpost points to the track across the common and down to Fort Warden, which is now a holiday centre. During the Second World War part of the common was cleared for use as allotments. Although no gorse remains on Colwell Common, 'Gorse Hill' still exists.

20. H.M.S. Gladiator 1908. One of the worst naval disasters off the Island was that in which H.M.S. Gladiator, second class cruiser, bound for Portsmouth, was rammed in the Solent off Yarmouth by the American liner St. Paul with the loss of twenty-seven of the crew, including one officer. The disaster occurred in the early afternoon of Saturday April 25th, 1908 during a blinding snow storm. The Gladiator began to heel over and heavier loss of life was prevented by beaching the vessel as quickly as possible off Black Rock, just inside Fort Victoria Pier. Magnificent rescue work was carried out by members of the Royal Engineers stationed at the fort. The Admiralty presented the officers and men of the 22nd Company Royal Engineers with a silver salver and the Gladiator's galley which had been restored, in recognition of the effective rescue work. Efforts to raise the Gladiator continued throughout the summer and the cruiser was refloated on October 3rd and towed to Portsmouth.

21. The gentleman who sent this card, which arrived in Freshwater on January 4th, 1903, left his home in Freshwater Bay for the Falkland Islands, with the object of exploring the possibilities of establishing a sheep station on the Islands. On the reverse side of the card three corners have been franked with the Freshwater Station stamp, the fourth bears a penny red Queen Victoria Falkland Islands stamp and a posting date of December 1902.

22. Colwell Bay circa 1906, situated on the north side of the West Wight. This beach owes its popularity to the long stretch of sand, good bathing and boating facilities for the visitor and its unsophisticated surroundings. In the background stands Fort Albert, built around 1857 as part of the defences of the Solent and containing at that time twenty-nine guns. This fort standing on the water's edge has now been converted into penthouses, commanding extensive views of the shipping in the Solent. The tracks spanning the large concrete blocks, as shown in the foreground of the picture, were used for the unloading of the heavy cannon circa 1890, which were then mounted on to gun-carts with iron wheels not much larger than a car wheel, but about a foot wide to help preventing them from sinking into the ground when making the perilous journeys to the various forts, using heavy horses borrowed from local farmers.

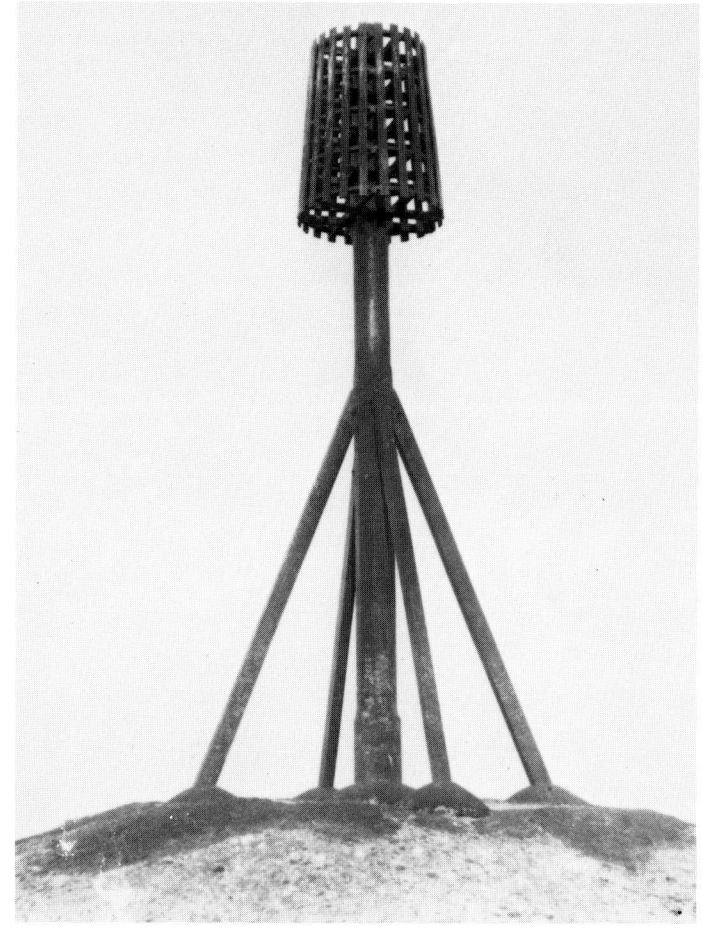

23. The Beacon circa 1897. On the highest part of Tennyson's Down stood Farringford Beacon, sometimes referred to as Nodes Beacon, the cliffs here rising to the height of 483 feet above sea-level. This Beacon only served as a landmark by day, for no light was displayed upon its turret at night. However, serving another purpose it was used as the 'visitors book' of this locality, the supports and even the turf around having been cut and carved with the names or initials of the Poet Laureate's numerous admirers. Looking at the picture one can pick out several letters. The Beacon was removed from this site, to make way for the new Tennyson Monument. However, to mark the Anniversary of the Queen's Silver Jubilee in 1977, the West Wight Rotary Club erected a reduced scale replica of the Beacon at the foot of the High Down, where it could not be seen from the sea. This model was voluntarily built by craftsmen in the employment of Messrs. W.F. Broomfield Ltd., and at the side stands all that remains from the old structure. (Photo A.H. Kirk.)

24. Tennyson's Cross 1897. This cross stands on the site formally occupied by the Nodes Beacon. It is constructed of Cornish granite and stands thirty-eight feet high – the choice of the memorial having been made by the late Poet's son Hallam Lord Tennyson. Local farmers with their heavy horses made the tedious journey to the downs with the stone. On August 6th, 1897, the birthday of Alfred Lord Tennyson, the Dean of Westminster unveiled the handsome Ionic cross which bears the following inscription: 'In memory of Alfred Lord Tennyson This Cross is raised, A Beacon to Sailors, By the People of Freshwater and other friends in England and America.' (Photo A.H. Kirk.)

25. Tennyson's Farm circa 1905, always referred to by the poet as 'The Home Farm'. The long stone cottage, with a deep thatch and old barns around it, lies at the foot of the kitchen garden, where Tennyson made an arbour for his wife in the early days of their coming to Freshwater. Here he and his wife used to sit and admire the white lilac, one of the poet's favourite flowers. A Mrs. Diment lived in the cottage about 1905 where she kept a 'large family' of hens, ducks, Guinea-fowl and peacocks. Of interest are the thatching spars soaking in the farm pond, weighted down with heavy stones.

26. Dimbola circa 1926. The home for about fourteen years of Mrs. Julia Margaret Cameron, born in Calcutta 1815, dying in Ceylon in 1879. It was about 1860 when she settled in Freshwater and first took up photography. Having purchased two houses, she afterwards joined them together by a castellated tower. It was not long before Dimbola Lodge was ivy clad and surrounded by shrubs. The Camerons were great friends of the Tennysons, therefore Mrs. Cameron was able to photograph most of the Poet's important guests. She worked diligently and achieved much publicity and success as a pioneer of photography. It would appear that relatives and followers dedicated to the arts occupied a large part of the area between Freshwater Bay and the Briary at Middleton, which was built by G.F. Watts the artist.

27. Norton Green — Annual Outing circa 1925. Life centred round the Mission Hall in this little hamlet. Built of natural stone in 1917, a brick extension was added at a later date. Each Sunday the bell rang to remind the children it was time for Sunday School, which was conducted by the Misses Everett, who lived in the neighbouring house. These two ladies organised meetings and events for many years. There were games evenings for both boys and girls, social evenings for all, Christmas parties and of course the annual outings, for which money could be paid in weekly. The mothers' meeting took place one afternoon a week, conducted by the ladies of St. Andrew's Church, finishing with 'a cup of tea and a bun'. Meetings of the Men's Brotherhood took place in the hall, which was also used as a polling station when necessity arose. As the children grew up and mostly left the Green, the changing pattern of life caused the decline of the Mission Hall, which has now been converted into a private dwelling.

28. An outing to Colwell 1925. This photograph was taken at 'Rectory Corner' Stroud, and the people shown in the picture used to spend their holidays in the stone cottage behind the Parish Hall, alongside the Old Rectory in Victoria Road. Nearby stands Stroud House, where in 1899 the death occurred of Mr. Arthur Tennyson, aged eighty-five, the last but one of the five brothers of the late Poet Laureate, to whom he bore a striking resemblance. This part of Victoria Road was quite a flourishing shopping centre in 1890. Alongside the crocus field there was Mr. Jones the butcher. Next came Wellington's chemist and newsagents (with hair cutting rooms), then Grantham's gents' outfitters (also boot and shoe warehouse). Also there were Leicester's — grocers, Wilson — sadler, Smith the oil merchant, china and ironmongery, who supplied oil to Farringford, and lastly Makings — milliners and dressmakers. The area is now completely residential, but Mr. Jones' butchers shop can be recognised by the coloured bricks.

7 FRESHWATER BAY (Isle of Wight). — After a storm.

29. Freshwater Bay — After a storm 1916. Driven during a furious gale past dangerous rocks at Freshwater Bay on November 5th, a large fullrigged 1,800 tons sailing ship, named 'Carl', grounded so close inshore that her crew of twenty-five were able to escape along the bowsprit on to the lawn of Glenbrook at the Bay. The crew were taken to Mrs. Dowty at the Temperance Hotel (no rum there) where they remained for several days. The ship remained in this position for about eleven months before being towed away. Explosives were used to blow a gap in the natural bar of rock which stretches across the bay, enabling the 'Carl' to be towed through to the open sea. One can see that the promenade is beginning to break up again, partly due to the battering by the 'Carl' before she came to rest. In this same year coastal flotsam produced kegs of rum, collected by local fishermen and handed over to the Authorities!

30. The Mall, Gate Lane, Freshwater Bay circa 1909. The Mall opposite the thatched church runs as far as the junction of Victoria Road and Bedbury Lane. Halfway along the Mall there was, at the turn of the century, a most interesting shop occupied by a Mr. Gubbins, who was official piano tuner to Queen Victoria at Osborne. Apart from a library agency his stock in trade included artists' materials, fancy goods, bookbinding, printing and a news agency. He also sold pianos, music and pictures, whilst on the forecourt stood a line of basinettes for hire to visitors. The shop on the Mall is still there, part of which is the Freshwater Bay Post Office, transferred from Orchard Bros. in the 1950's. To the left of the junction runs the Primrose path or Tennyson Lane. Following this path and turning left at the little rustic bridge, brings one to the foot of the downs where it is only a short climb to the summit before descending to Watcombe and Freshwater Bays.

31. The Causeway, Freshwater circa 1897. This lovely view has changed very little since the turn of the century. The Parish Church is situated behind the trees, to the right of the old stone cottage. The Freshwater to Newport railway line crossed the road approaching the bridge, the gates being manually operated by the crossing keeper, who lived in a tiny cottage alongside the track. There used to be a small wooden footbridge for pedestrians, but this was replaced with a 'kissing gate' in 1916. During the severe storms in 1916 the sea wall at Freshwater Bay was breached; the sea broke through flooding the whole of the Yar valley. The railway embankment was washed away and the water reached within inches of the ceiling in the Level Crossing Keeper's cottage.

32. Memorial Service, Freshwater Church 1910. The news of the death of King Edward VII on May 6th plunged the Island into mourning for a much loved Monarch. Having spent a good deal of his childhood at Osborne, and his love of the sea made him closely connected with the Island. This Memorial Service, with the parade and inspection of the Island Volunteers, took place about May 20th. The building on the right of the foreground was the old malthouse, owned by Mr. John Emberly, a brewer of Church Place in 1883.

33. The year 1922 saw the removal of Lloyd's Bank Ltd., from the Solicitor's Offices, as shown in the background, to its present position at the junction of Queen's Road and Tennyson Road. Previously the newly converted premises had been a butcher's shop. Next door to the Bank in Tennyson Buildings, built in 1893, there was a Social Club, as worded on the lantern outside. Then comes the Boot Store, where they gave 'sterling value for ready mades' and carried out repairs with 'neatness and tenacity'. (Photo A.H. Kirk.)

34. Kingsbridge, Freshwater 1901. The funeral procession of soldiers killed at Fort Redoubt, Freshwater Bay, where a terrible accident occurred on June 25th. During competitive firing, the breach-block of a 12 pounder quick-firing gun blew out, killing Capt. A. Le Messurier Bray, staff instructor of gunnery, three members of the Artillery gun team and injuring six other members, including Col. Nixon R.A., commanding the forces in the Island. The cortege is shown proceeding along Brookfield Road towards the Station, on its way to Hook Hill and the Parish Church. The building behind the flagpole was the letter sorting office for the Old Post Office and the little low building beyond was 'Poodle Cooper's' Blacksmith's shop.

35. Needles and Lighthouse circa 1909. When the Trinity Board erected the new lighthouse on the most westerly rock in 1858, a base of sixty feet in diameter had to be levelled for the foundations. The granite blocks used for the structure were prepared at Totland Bay, where a wooden Pier had been built for purposes connected with the construction of the lighthouse. A Mr. Barchard was appointed lighthouse keeper and on the night of January 1st, 1859 the first friendly warning light was seen. Previously the old lighthouse stood on the Needles Down, in which Argand Lamps (a burner admitting air within a cylindrical flame) were used, but the light was often obscured by fog. A large bell, weighing nearly two tons, was erected at the Needles lighthouse in 1896, to warn mariners in foggy weather. The former Needles battery and rocket testing sites are now open to the public, where recently, an interesting museum has been established. (Photo A.H. Kirk.)

36. Alum Bay Pier circa 1906. The man walking along the pier towards the camera, Mr. C. Calloway, worked at the Royal Needles Hotel, which was destroyed by fire on the 20th February 1910 and was not rebuilt. Pleasure boats from Yarmouth visited Alum Bay, where passengers could disembark at the pier to buy souvenirs and collect samples of the renowned coloured sands. However, during the early part of the Second World War, the middle section of the pier was demolished as a deterrent to enemy landings. Eventually the rest disintegrated. Above the coloured cliffs is a monument paying tribute to Marconi's success after he set up the first Wireless Transmitting Station in the world in 1897. The station handled its first paid message in 1898 and in the same year, the new-fangled wireless received Royal Patronage with Queen Victoria using it to keep in touch with the Prince of Wales, who was aboard the Royal Yacht.

37. Headen Hall circa 1909. Situated on the west side of Alum Bay, these premises were always referred to as the 'Squire's House'. A Mr. Squire rented the Cliffs of Headen Hill for several years, the sands being of considerable economic value, their whiteness and purity rendering them particularly suitable for the making of glass. The cliffs were extensively worked and Mr. Squire recorded that between 1850 and 1855 nearly twenty-two thousand tons were shipped from Yarmouth, principally to the Bristol and London Glass Houses. The sand for shipment was stored in the 'Sand House' nearby Yarmouth Bridge. This old stone building is now part of Hayles Yacht Repairing business. (Photo A.H. Kirk.)

38. Freshwater Parish Church circa 1895. Dedicated to 'All Saints' this handsome church has, in one form or another, been keeping a watchful eye over the village for about nine hundred years. The oldest part of the church is the south-east Chapel, built in the eleventh century after the Norman Conquest. Two further chapels were added in the thirteenth century, whilst the close of the fifteenth century saw the addition of north and south porches, which were lost in the restoration of 1874. In some of the earlier pictures one can see the Elizabethan windows. In the south wall of the South Chapel there is a Sepulchral recess monument designed for the interment of Richard de Afton, successor to William de Afton, who held the manor circa 1224. There are some interesting monuments in the church to the Tennyson Family, who worshipped here for many years. (Photo A.H. Kirk.)

39. The year 1914. Unloading Shingles from Tanner's Barge at Kings Manor jetty. This is one of the lovely views encountered whilst walking along the bridle path, through Becketts copse towards Yarmouth, formerly the old railway line, and what a delight it is to be here. There are many sea and fresh water birds on the river, their calls competing with the song of the land birds in the copse, whilst above, amongst the pines, the red squirrels scamper. In the early spring the copse is yellow with primroses, the colour gradually changing with the arrival of the bluebells. Looking back towards the bridge, silhouetted against the sky, is the Parish Church and the noble range of downland between Freshwater and the Needles, presented to the nation by Hallam Lord Tennyson in 1927 in memory of his illustrious father, the Poet Laureate.

40. Queen's Road circa 1908 from opposite the drive of Middleton House, an eighteenth century building with several later additions. The 'monkey tree' as shown is still in existence and beyond is a well preserved attractive shop front with its coloured and pictured tiling. The following building is now the Conservative Club then the road leads to Brookfield Corner. In the foreground behind the trees on the right is where, on the 31st August 1906, Sir Godfrey Baring M.P. opened the new Council School, accommodating one hundred and fifty children. This school was considerably enlarged in 1939 and has now become the Freshwater Middle School.

41. The opening of the Soldiers Club, erected at the junction of High Street and Avenue Road, took place on May 3rd, 1915. This facility must have been a welcome change from barrack room life for the soldiers stationed in the area. The Royal Warwickshire Regiment is shown complete with band, also represented were members of the Guides and Scouts. The site of the old club is now occupied by the commodious West Wight Social Club.

42. Station Road and Station, Freshwater 1913. Before one reaches the auction rooms, which are still in operation, is the Freshwater Pumping Station, the sewerage scheme having been completed in May 1905, after many difficulties and much opposition. Gillings the Bakery and Restaurant is now a laundrette. The Pet shop is still looking after the needs of the numerous domestic animals, having extended into the next shop which, for many years, had been an ironmongers. At the far end was Mr. Wilson the saddler, who closed down his business quite a long time ago. After the demolition of the Station premises, a new factory, known as the Acorn Spring Works, was built on the site. The old Signal Box, having been salvaged, was erected as a bus shelter on the right of the picture towards the corner. However, some time after, railway enthusiasts managed to get the box transferred to the Haven Street Railway Museum where it has been 'lovingly restored'.

43. Golden Hill Fort circa 1909. There are several attractive footpaths around the perimeter of the old fort, commanding beautiful views of the Afton and Tennyson Downs, the Yar Valley, Hurst Castle and beyond. These footpaths lead one through the woods to different parts of the village. Originally the fort, camouflaged in Golden Gorse, was the Headquarters of Coastal Defence for the West Wight, the windmill, with a well of 173 feet below, taking charge of the water supply. When the War Department had no further use for the old batteries, the various forts were sold and this one now houses several small industrial businesses. However, fortunately for Freshwater, the Council acquired the land for use as a public Park, where several tree planting ceremonies took place; some of these trees having matured quite well whilst others, unfortunately, became the victims of vandals. (Photo A.H. Kirk.)

44. Colwell Bay Bathing Belles circa 1916. Before the turn of the century this Bay was very little visited, there being only a narrow lane through the Chine to the beach. The cliffs here are most interesting, being composed of layers of clay, and sandstone full of fossil shells and partially covered with long grass. It is possible to walk westward along the sea wall, past the old Ford Warden to Totland Bay. Walking in the other direction would take one past the Forts Albert and Victoria, then on to Norton Spit where the sand is soft and silvery and a little ferry boat makes trips across Yarmouth Harbour.

45. Compton Manor Farm circa 1905. Travelling over the Military Hill from Freshwater Bay for about two and a half miles, one descends towards Compton where lies ahead this attractive old farm, nestling in a hollow at the foot of the downs. The deeds of the farm lands have been traced back to William the Conquerer. However, in circa 1431 the owners were the De Compton family and there is a fifteenth century brass to Adam de Compton in the Freshwater Parish Church. The present occupier and his family have been operating the farm for over sixty years, the dairy herd, pigs and poultry forming part of the holding, together with the different herds of Black Galloways, which have been grazing the downs behind the Farm for about thirty years. With them were two old horses put out to grass – one of them reaching the ripe old age of thirty-seven. (Photo A.H. Kirk.)

46. Florist's Shop, High Street, circa 1909. There has been a florist's shop on these premises for about a hundred years, the road having been called hops Hill before it became known as the High Street, where a Mr. Fry was in business in 1883. Here we see the loading of potted geraniums into Mr. Cooper's horse drawn van. Geraniums, one of the present owners specialities, are still being loaded into delivery vans of a different era. Heathfield House in Heathfield Road, a continuation of the High Street, was built as a holiday home for Mr. Bradley, who in 1881 became Dean of Westminster. The Bradleys were great friends of the Tennysons, the children spending much time in both Farringford and Heathfield. Following the road to the junction and turning right, brings one to the former Church of St. Andrew, Norton.

47. Totland Bay Hotel circa 1902. For a hundred years this hotel stood overlooking the lovely Bay of Totland — then the bulldozers arrived. It opened in 1880 and was described as 'a fine noble brick building of modern construction, fitted with every comfort and convenience, with an ample supply of the Purest Spring Water from the neighbouring downs'. The Proprietor was one of the promoters who, in 1901, put forward a scheme for a Solent Tunnel at the western end of the Island. This Scheme, although welcomed by the County Council and other public authorities, failed to materialise. During the Second World War the hotel was mobilised as a hospital, where wounded from the French beaches were brought. There is still good safe bathing at Totland Bay and the walk along the cliffs round Hatherwood Point towards the Needles is most exciting and colourful, especially when the heather is in bloom.

48. Lych-gate, Christ Church, Totland, circa 1909. Entrance to the Churchyard is by the Lych-gate which was designed by Percy Stone, whose work 'Architectural Antiquities of the Isle-of Wight' is much sought after by historians. The superstructure is the work of J.H. King, an Island Craftsman of Blackwater. Mrs. H.W. Burnett donated the gate in memory of her husband, who died in 1906 and was for many years closely connected with the church. On the 10th March 1906 this gate was dedicated by the Bishop of Winchester. One may wonder why it was erected in such an unusual position relative to the church. This was accomplished with the assumption that a further extension would follow, thereby bringing the gate in alignment.

49. Totland Bay circa 1904. Scenes like this may fascinate us today, but in the past they must have been a bit of an 'eyesore', especially to the 'gentry' who chose the West Wight in which to build their country houses for the 'lovely, lonely bays, innocent of lodginghouse or bathing machine!' The iron pier, built in 1880, forming a pleasant promenade for the visitor and a bazaar, well stocked with shells, fossils and ornaments made from Alum Bay sands, provided an added attraction. A few yards from where this picture was taken, stood a lifeboat station from which the 'Dove' lifeboat operated, this boat having been acquired by public subscription in 1878 and voluntarily manned. In 1884 a new house was built and the RNLI provided a lifeboat named 'Charles Luccombe'. This station continued to operate until 1924, when Yarmouth was selected as the Lifeboat Station for the West Wight and supplied with a motor lifeboat.

50. Christ Church, Totland Bay circa 1895. The church, erected in 1874/75, was a neat edifice built of natural stone, from a local quarry, in the Early English style of Architecture with a spiral tower and one bell. Over its comparatively short life-span the church has undergone many important alterations and additions. At one stage the tower was removed and positioned on a stone base alongside the old octagonal vestry on the north-east side, where the bell was operated by hand. This base is still in existence. In 1869 a temporary church of wood was erected in York Road, where services were conducted until 1875 when the new church was completed. This wooden structure was later resited on Totland Beach as a library and reading room.

51. Afton Manor circa 1880. Like other manors on the Isle of Wight the deeds have been traced back to before the Norman Conquest. The Urry family held the manor for about two hundred years and thereafter the house and lands changed hands many times. Here we see the Manor House with its attractive covering of ivy and the magnificent tree standing in front, at present trying very hard to survive. The procedure of grass cutting with the aid of a donkey was widely used before the introduction of more sophisticated machines. The present owner has been in residence for about twelve years. Being a vintage car enthusiast, he has now established a permanent home for his 'relics of the past' at the Exhibition Centre, Calbourne. Although the previous owner of the Manor had a gleaming Rolls Royce 'rugged up' in one of the outbuildings, he was more interested in four legs rather than four wheels, being the proud owner of the 1922 Grand National Winner 'Music Hall', finally put out to grass in the Manor fields.

52. Flooding in Freshwater 1921. Showing one of Bert Hall's Carriers negotiating the water whilst making his daily run into Newport, watched by two local lads, Nobby Clark and Mark Carrol. A similar occurrence was experienced in the 1950's when three inches of rain fell in an hour. After this incident the storm drains were enlarged and the brook widened, this operation having since proved adequate. The brook emerges from under the road where the posts are seen and follows its course behind the houses to Bowbridge and the Yar Valley. To the left of the big tree are Veasey Cottages and the lane leading past the National School to Longhalves.

53. Winter in Freshwater circa 1915. The small boy pulling the sledge is Jack Dall, now almost an octogenarian, who very kindly loaned some of his pictures. The Palace was formerly the Assembly Hall where in 1904 Lord Tennyson attended a civic reception on the completion of his service as Governor General of Australia. The Palace opened about 1915 and provided film and stage shows as well as dances, until the late 1920's when it was destroyed by fire, being replaced by a draper's and outfitter's shop. The late 1930's saw the erection of the Regent Cinema on the opposite side of the road where the trees once stood. With a midweek change of programme, this cinema proved very popular for some years, but as television became more widespread, the audiences dwindled and this led to the closure and demolition of the Regent, leaving a site for the inevitable supermarket.

54. Freshwater Cricket Team, Afton Park 1900. For about thirty years the Cotton family owned the Georgian Manor House, which stood in the Park, and a number of headstones to this family may be seen in the Parish Churchyard. When a Mr. Tankard purchased the property circa 1899, he established a cricket pitch in the grounds and insisted that his staff should play, in fact it is said that he would not engage men unless they agreed. In Afton Park a large pit was opened to supply ballast during the construction of the railway. The pit showed about six feet of gravel, but yielded no fossils.

55. Four-in-hand circa 1909. 'Magnet', the local excursion coach, taking day trippers to various parts of the Island. One of the most popular trips was a day at the Ashey Races, some sixteen miles away, with a brief stop in Newport. The driver was Mr. H. Cooper, whilst Mr. Sweet, standing, was the guard who had a seat and a brake at the back of the coach. The guard was also responsible for positioning the 'drag-shoe', which hung on a chain underneath the coach. This was an iron shoe which when placed under the wheel, prevented it from rotating when descending a steep hill. Before the railway came to the West Wight, there were two four horse coach routes marked on the map, one to Newport from Alum Bay, and one to Ventnor via Shalcombe, Hulverstone, Brighstone, Shorwell, Chale and then along the coast to Ventnor. There was not a Military Road at that time and two journeys a week were made along these routes.

56. The year 1911. Unfortunately marred by the rain, celebrations took place at School Green Freshwater for the Coronation of King George V on 22nd June. There was a general holiday and much rejoicing throughout the Island. Beacons on the downs flashed the news 'The King is crowned', whilst off shore lay a wonderful naval pageant with flags of eighteen sea powers fluttering in the breeze. Commemorative Medals were presented by the Royal Governor, Princess Henry of Battenberg, to schoolchildren of the Wight.

57. School Green circa 1880. Showing the two thatched cottages used as the local school until about 1850. These cottages were demolished to make way for new development which took place in 1896, and a stone dated 1767 from the old building was incorporated in the new building as a memorial to the former School House. The Wesleyan Chapel was demolished at a much later date and replaced by the present Wesley Hall in Brookfield Road.

58. Moa Place circa 1903. Showing the row of buildings and shops built in 1896 on the site of the demolished cottages and named Moa Place. Moa is a great wingless extinct New Zealand bird similar to an emu. It was alive within the last two hundred and fifty years, for in the British Museum are some feathers in a chief's weapon brought from New Zealand by Capt. Cook and identified as having belonged to this bird. The houses on the right also have New Zealand names such as Hokitika, Wanganui, Oamarue, and Timarue Place. One can see in the picture the 'Coronation Oak', planted in 1901 to mark the crowning of Edward VII.

59. Photograph taken circa 1926 of Girl Guides and Brownies in the grounds of Norton Lodge, Norton, the home of the Hollins family, who were connected with the Viyella Firm. Four of the daughters are represented in the picture, one being the Commissioner and another the Captain. In the 1930's the house and grounds were sold and developed as a holiday camp.

60. The Star Inn, Camp Road, Freshwater circa 1904. Formerly a dwelling house, changing to the Star Inn during the second half of the last century. Apart from the locals, the inn was also a popular rendezvous for troops stationed in the area. During the First World War beer was very scarce and whenever there was a delivery, the landlord would hoist a Union Jack which could be seen by the soldiers at Golden Hill Fort. One can imagine the response! However, during the 1939-1945 campaign, the large Saloon of the Star was commandeered by the Army and used as their Head Quarters when manoeuvres with the British and Canadian Forces were taking place. The lane alongside the inn leads to New Village where stood the Bricklayers Arms, occupied in 1888 by a James Downer. Both these inns are now private dwellings.

61. Norton from the Bridge circa 1919. After crossing the bridge from Yarmouth, having paid a toll of one penny, Norton was soon reached and described as a pleasant but scattered village. The toll was abolished in 1934 after the County Council purchased the bridge. Following the road until the end of the railings, brings one to a lane leading to the River Yar Boatyard, formerly the site of the old gasworks and gasometer, a footpath then continues as far as the Parish Church and the Red Lion Inn. According to an old Directory in 1859, a William Sawley occupied the inn.

62. Gate Lane, Freshwater Bay in the 1920's shows Richardsons the chemists, Laceys the grocers and Starks Hotel, which is today still covered in creeper, giving a beautiful display of colour in the autumn, especially when seen from the foot of the downs opposite. The wall on the left of the picture is part of Bakers Farm, no longer farmed, but the remains of the old barns are to be seen from the footpath alongside St. Agnes Church. It was the Bakers with whom Mrs. Cameron, the photographer friend of Lord Tennyson, travelled when she left Freshwater for Ceylon where they had coffee plantations. Following the devastation through disease of the coffee growing areas, tea planting was substituted.

63. Longhalves, Freshwater circa 1909. About a hundred yards southwards from the Parish Church there is on the right, between the houses, a narrow path known as Longhalves. This path stretches for nearly a mile, but provides a shorter distance for the parishioners to and from the village. About half-way along stand the three little thatched cottages as shown with their respective wash-houses nearby. These have now been combined into one dwelling. In the far cottage lived the village midwife and it would be this path she would use if called out to houses in and around Church Place. The village end of Longhalves finishes between Bank Buildings, where Mr. Small had his Dental Practice for many years, and the Vine Hotel.

THE APPROACH TO COLWELL BAY I.W. (SHOWING HURST CASTLE IN THE DISTANCE)

64. Colwell Bay circa 1928. A dead calm sea and people just ambling on the beach conveys to one a feeling of relaxation on approaching the bay. The tide indicator provided useful information to the holiday maker. In this year a repeated suggestion of a Solent Tunnel in the area was unfavourably received by the Ministry of Transport, there being no reason to anticipate such an increase in traffic as to justify the expenditure. Hurst Castle, shown in the distance, is situated at the end of a long bank of shingle, or probably clay flints, extending in a curved line nearly two miles from the Hampshire coast. It was originally one of Henry VIII's forts, consisting of a tower with a date 1535, flanked by a long granite wall, with embrasures for heavy guns. It was here where King Charles I was confined for twenty-seven days after his seizure by the army at Newport on 1st December 1648.

65. The Road to Totland Bay circa 1906. From the ground near the pier entrance and across the little bridge one reaches the narrow strip of pine screened down turf at the top of the cliff, known as the Turf Walk. This is a lovely tranquil walk, commanding fine views of the Solent. There is an interesting descent to the shore, about a hundred yards beyond the end of the turf, which leads to the old lifeboat station, where to the west the unspoilt area attracts a variety of bird life, the whitethroats having been observed on several occasions.

66. Circa 1911, The Isle of Wight Rifles, formerly the Island Volunteers, leaving the Drill Hall, Freshwater for a parade. The Unit, formed in 1859, had several changes of name; in 1885 it was renamed The 5th (I.W. Princess Beatrice's) Volunteer Battalion of the Hampshire Regiment, with H.R.H. Prince Henry of Battenberg as honorary Colonel. In 1892 the Prince with his regiment marched from Albany Barracks, Parkhurst to Freshwater and took part in a long field day. On the following day he was with the regiment in a 'night attack' on Freshwater. Prince Henry died in January 1896 whilst serving with the military expedition to Ashanti. The Island contributed nearly ten thousand men to the war forces during the 1914-1918 conflict, about one fifth of them never to return. The war memorials at Freshwater Church and Cokes Green, Totland give the names of those who gave their lives.

21 FRESHWATER. — (Isle of Wight). — General View. — LL.

67. Freshwater Bay circa 1912. Tennis parties played an important part of the social life in Freshwater and Totland during the early part of the 1900's. Most of the large private houses had courts and some belonging to the letting houses were offered for hire until about the early 1930's. This picture was taken from Glenbrook and shows the old coastguard cottages, built in 1875, just behind the Temperance Hotel (now Saunders) and to the left Marine House, Ocean View and Afton Down House. During the 1939-1945 War a bomb fell in the Square, just behind Marine House, and destroyed The Porch, once the home of Lady Anne Ritchie, writer daughter of W.M. Thackeray and friend of the Tennyson family.

68. Circa 1928. Boy Scouts on Parade, marching along Avenue Road towards the Drill Hall, carrying their new staves for the first time. The Group (the second oldest in the Island) held their meetings in the Rover Hut, School Green, now referred to by the locals as the 'Black Hut'. Mr. Green was scoutmaster and Mr. Jeffreys the area scoutmaster. The Rover Group, formed with the encouragement of Lord Baden Powell, became the largest in the South of England and it was the Rovers who first introduced the local fire service about 1926/27, practicing with a borrowed manual pump from Newport. Equipment was then purchased from the Ventnor Urban District Council, followed by the aquisition of a fire engine about 1936/37.

69. The Parade Totland Bay circa 1908. Unfortunately due to coast erosion there is now only about half the distance shown from Beach House to the railings. This house was used for summer letting and has stood up to the elements remarkably well. The flag flying on the cliff indicates the location of a coastguard station. Here is a good example of dress during the early part of the century, the little push chair would have been made from cane.

70. The year 1915. First Aid practice, combined with the Red Cross, regularly took place at the National School during the First World War, together with night exercises when the 'wounded' were located and brought in for treatment.

71. Needles Lighthouse circa 1930. The Staff of the present lighthouse consists of a Principal Keeper and two Assistant Keepers, who work one month at the lighthouse and with one month off duty. Reliefs are effected by Trinity House Tender or by local boat. The range of light is seventeen miles, the intensity 35,000 candle power and the fog signal sounds twice every thirty seconds with a range of four sea miles. Each year the Yarmouth lifeboat takes Christmas Fayre to the men on duty, effecting a landing if the weather permits, otherwise rocket apparatus has to be used. This apparatus, having been invented by a Carisbrook man named Dennett, was used in 1890 when thirty-six lives were saved from the three masted ship 'Irex', which had been driven onto the rocks in Scratchell's Bay.

72. The Vine Hotel circa 1921. At one time the building did have a vine growing over it, but here it is covered with creeper giving that attractive old world appearance. The board displayed on the fence is the bus time table for the Vectis Bus Company (before it became Southern Vectis), whose services were spreading throughout the island helped along by the coal strike which caused the train services to be suspended. The shops on the left of the picture were built on the site of Cliff Hall, a house which was destroyed by fire and the bay window above the horse rider was knocked off by a double decker bus when they were first introduced into the area.

73. This 1925 photograph shows Miss Waistell and her girls when they won the Royal Governor's shield for the annual competition of the Red Cross Teams, resumed after the 1914-1918 War. It was Miss Waistell to whom in 1925 May Lady Tennyson presented the money for an urgently needed ambulance in the West Wight, so much valuable time having been lost in the past whilst waiting for an ambulance to come from Newport. Princess Beatrice, the Governor of the Island, presented the newly acquired Riley vehicle, named the May Lady Tennyson Ambulance, to Miss Waistell at a dedication ceremony which took place at the Drill Hall. The ambulance service was run and maintained by a body of voluntary workers, for twenty-three years organising many different money making project until 1961 when the running of the ambulance was taken over by the Rotarians.

74. Circa 1906. Celebrating the end of the Harvest with the Master, guests and workers having a picnic tea; thought to be in the fields of Freshwater Farm. Very nice examples of the starched white aprons are shown. Perhaps somebody may identify these people – the sailor in the foreground looking incredibly like Edward VII.

75. A late 1890's picture of a local family showing the type of clothing worn by the average person during this period. These were the 'Sunday best' clothes, a custom which continued until the 1930's. The lace collars and accessories are much sought after by collectors and popular with the fashions of today.